T0167033

Poems From the Heart of a Woman

Glenda Bagley and Lovella Bagley

Cover designed by: Willis Bagley

iUniverse, Inc.
Bloomington

Poems From the Heart of a Woman

iUniverse books may be ordered through booksellers or by contacting:

iUniverse
1663 Liberty Drive
Bloomington, IN 47403
www.iuniverse.com
1-800-Authors (1-800-288-4677)

Because of the dynamic nature of the Internet, any web addresses or links contained in this book may have changed since publication and may no longer be valid. The views expressed in this work are solely those of the author and do not necessarily reflect the views of the publisher, and the publisher hereby disclaims any responsibility for them.

Any people depicted in stock imagery provided by Thinkstock are models, and such images are being used for illustrative purposes only.

Certain stock imagery © Thinkstock.

ISBN: 978-1-4759-4150-0 (sc)
ISBN: 978-1-4759-4151-7 (e)

Printed in the United States of America

iUniverse rev. date: 9/26/2012

Contents

Background Information

This book has poetry that my mother wrote years ago. Most people with Alzheimer's disease lose their memory. Lovella Bagley is a woman of faith who served her family and her community and church. She is a kind woman who often helped others in need. In our small town of Lubbock, Texas she was known for her good deeds and services to people within our community. As a tribute to her in her faith in Jesus Christ I have complied her poetry in hopes that others will learn about her life. In other words, I hope that you will get to know Lovella through her poetry.

Lee and Lovella Bagley in happier times posing with their grandson and his wife. Right to left Lovella Jennifer, Jason, Lee Earnest Bagley Sr.

Also I would like to take this opportunity to allow you (the reader) to accept Jesus Christ into your heart. God will heal your mind, body and spirit and he will guide you. But most of all, he will give you the gift of eternal life. You must be born again and accept Jesus Christ into your heart.

In John3:16 the bible says, For God so loved the world that he gave his only begotten son that whosoever beliveth in him shall not perish but have eternal life. If you would like to become a Christian say this prayer:

> Lord I invite you into my heart and I accept you as my savior and Lord. I believe that you died on the cross for me. I believe you shed your blood for my sins. That one day I will have the gift of eternal life In Jesus name I pray Amen. It's that simple now; you need to read your bible every day. Become a member of a local church and fellowship with other Christians.

Acknowledgements

Writing a book any kind of book can be difficult I would like to thank my family. It is a long a tedious process to say the least. From conception to completion writing a book is no easy task. I would like to thank Jesus Christ my Lord and savior for inspiring me. One of my favorite verses in the bible says, it best.

In Phil. 4:13, I can do all things through Christ who strengthens me.

Special thanks: My parents Lee Earnest Bagley Sr. & Lovella Bagley for being good role models for me and my siblings. I will always be grateful for all the sacrifices you made for me. Brenda Davis, Willis Bagley for their words of encouragement. In addition: I would like to thank my friend Adorfus Bell who encouraged me and everyone that supported with prayers and or kind words. May God Bless you for your kindness in my time of need.

Dedication

This book is dedicated to my loving mother. Lovella Bagley who had a dream to become a writer. She was the mother of 10 children and 15 grandchildren and 3 great- grandchildren.

My mother worked as a housekeeper and a cook for Plainsman Hotel located in Lubbock ,Texas. She married my father Lee Earnest Bagley Sr. in 1946. They were married for 65 years, Unfortunately, he passed away on December 12, 2009. My father was a plumber who worked for an apartment complex. He had a great sense of humor and a wonderful personality. In my upcoming book called "Why am I here? I will discuss in details about my family and our life. My mother was diagnosed with Alzheimer's disease at the age of seventy – five. I watched her go from a vibrant woman full of life to being in a wheelchair. I cried, as I saw the pain in her face when the doctor gave her the news. My mother never gave-up on her life-long goal to someday become a writer. So she continued writing in her journal every day her thoughts in poetic form.

Daily I watched her struggle with her ability to remember words, names, and everyday events. Each night she wrote poems and short stories and put her journal in a silver suitcase. Years passed and I my siblings became her caregiver. Somehow, I could not stop thinking about lost silver brief case. During this time we had relocated to Dallas, Texas. My brother Rodney decided to go to Lubbock, Texas to visit our relatives. He went to a storage unit to retrieve some old furniture. He walked to the back of the storage unit. In the back of the storage unit behind an old couch there it was! The Silver Suitcase" that I had been searching for everywhere. I was overjoyed to have the " Silver Suitcase" in my possession again. *Poems from the Heart of a Woman* showcases the poetry that Lovella has written along with a few of my poems.

Lee & Lovella Bagley took this photograph
shortly after being married in 1946.

Memories of my Father

The fondest memory I have of my father was the day, I cut my hair. When I was in the 7th grade I decided to perm my hair. Well, I left the chemical in my hair too long it was damaged. So I had to cut all of my hair off. I was so embarrassed my brothers teased me and called me funny names. No, not my father he just said, "You still look beautiful to me. That is just one of the great memories I have of my father. I wrote a poem for him entitled "Birthday Wish"

Birthday wish!

I don't' wish you had a big mansion or lots of land

Because where you are it's not a part of God's plan

I don't wish you had diamonds or a second – hand jewels

Or even a set of plumber's tools

I don't wish you had thousands of dollars or that you were a millionaire

Because where you are you won't need it there

But what I do wish is that you were here with me

I know it's not possible because you're with God and daddy, I know you are free

By Glenda Bagley

Say, Cheese! My father smiles while I take his picture. Happy 87th Birthday!

Lee and Lovella Bagley are sitting in the living room on Christmas Day. (2007)

My father is sharing a Thanksgiving dinner with his family.

My father is sitting on the balcony wearing his favorite hat.

Every body Smile!
Glenda and family at a graduation in Tyler Texas. (2007)

The first section of the book will have poetry written my mother by Lovella Bagley. All poems in the first section were composed by her.

My mother is a persistent person when she decides to do something no one can deter her. The poetry in this book reveals her innermost thoughts. I remember when I was a teenager and we wrote poetry together. It was fun competing with one another to see , who could compose the best poem. I did my best but somehow her poems were still better. Now things have changed and I miss the fun times we shared. She is in a wheelchair and no longer able to talk. But her spirit and faith in God is strong. "I am thankful mother, to have you in my life your loving daughter" Glenda Bagley

Me and my mother at my high school graduation in 1983.

This book is divided into 2 sections the first section has poetry written by Lovella Bagley. The second section in the book has a few poems written by me.

The saying goes that the apple doesn't fall too far from the tree is true. Many times I sit at my desk and write poetry. I enjoy writing on different topis; such as ,love nature,religion. Sometimes when I will write lyrics for songs. I guess, I truly am my mother's daughter.

Make Each Day Count

Make each day of life count

It doesn't matter in what amount

Do something good every day

As you pass along the way

If your personality is bad

And someone is always making you mad

Check yourself and do it now

And maybe you will find when to start

No better time to make a difference

Why not start now?

My mother hanging – out the laundry in the backyard.

Lovella is waiting for the candles to be
blown out on her cake. Happy Birthday!

Family members stand around her as Lovella looks away.

Lovella sitting alone at her birthday party.
Smile Mom!

I can't imagine

I can't imagine what's on a person' mind

When he goes around losing valuable time

What can one do to prove he's trustworthy and true?

Time is valuable you might say

For this is the last time that we will pass this way

Time is of the essence

If we want to receive God's blessings

We must start now and stop asking God

What, Where and Why?

I won't forget

I thank you for your hospitality

That you have shown today

I will always be in debt to you

In a kindly way

You turned aside from your busy schedule

And thought of me in my sorrow

I want you to know because of that

I won't forget your tomorrow

Living and Forgiving

There are things you may do wrong

Even though you think that you are right

And you're on your journey home

And if God takes a look into your heart

You would have to stop and make a new start

In these troubled times we live in

We must learn how to forgive

Even though it might seem hard

Each one has to do their part

You must somewhere make a start

The advice that you are getting might come from a sinner

For he is wrong and not a winner

If you read the word of God

Then he will show you where to start

Living and forgiving that's what God wants us to do

If you learn how to live and forgive

This is pleasing God and he in turn will forgive you

Angels are among us

God uses his angels to carry out his word

They bring the message from God above

Joy and tidings and bundles of love

Many times we wonder why

God's beautiful angels will pass us by

That is something we will know

When God himself opens the door

Angels never sleep they are busy both day and night

Carrying the message

Where God says some are sent to make you glad

They were never meant to make you mad or sad.

There is a path I must travel

There is a path

That one must travel on distant shore

Where peace and joy fill the air

And weeping shall be no more

Love ones and friends are there

Watching and waiting for our arrival

And life on this earth shall be ended

And time shall be no more

And when my feet step on those celestial shores

I'll see my loved ones standing there

Waiting for me

Something within

Will let me know that time

That has been shall be no more

Message

I received a message from an angel one day

God sent this, in strange kind of way

On beautiful summer morning while laying in my bed

I thought I saw an angel, standing at foot of my bed

And this angel stood dressed in dark

I was wondering if she knew what was in my heart

To my surprise

She stood there gazing into my eyes

I will never forget that day

I heard her wings flap as, she flew away

So I got on my knees and prayed that God would answer my prayer

I did not know he would, or if he really cared

I put my mom in the hospital only a few days before

Since I was sick in bed at home I really didn't know

One day while riding down the street

I heard a loud voice speaking to me

I thought that was neat

I know you are worried and filled with despair

But anything happens to your mother

You will be the one there

Not many days after that my mom said "Good bye

And went home to be with the Lord

To live with him in heaven

I think of her often

But I am not really alone

We will meet again someday

In a beautiful place called home

When the church bell rings

When the church bell rings out loud

People always look for a crowd

That is simply not the case

For God will always be there for you

Sharing your love and grace

As the preacher preaches the word

People talk so loud he can't be heard

If he says something to the congregation

He thinks is not right

Some members get upset and want to start a fight

But when he preaches there are some who fall asleep

He preaches and doesn't pay them any mind.

But he still gets talked about every time

Preachers bow on your knees and pray

Don't worry, try to forget what people may say

I Have Questions

As I sit here on a lovely summer's day

I realize that I needed answers to help me find my way

I am not being ignored, as they say

I just need someone to help me find my way

Living in a world like ours today,

It's hard to find your way, live for Jesus it's the only way

With so many bad things to do

Not only me, but also you

To think of someone to meet your demands

Why not try Jesus' plans

He will help you and he is in command

If you hope to be saved you must understand his plan

If I dedicate my service

If I dedicate my service my service to God

And do it with all my heart

If I hope to see his face

I must give him love, truth and praise

It doesn't matter how short

If we mean it from our hearts

We must do it his way

Or in his presence we can't stay

God must see our sincere heart

Then he will know that we are doing our part

If we be steadfast in our life

He won't have to tell us twice

Many times we think we are right

With Jesus in our life, it seems that eternity is not our sight

But if we are faithful to his call

There will be no reason to worry at all

If we humble down and pray

He will teach us what to say

For there is no other way

To be with God on Judgment day

I will sail away

After this life here is over,

I will sail away

And be where Jesus lives

That's where I like to stay

There is place where he lives

There will be no tears

And there will be more fears

God sent his son to the earth

To redeem all mankind

It doesn't make any difference

Whether they are white, black or brown

You can make it if you try

Just follow Jesus, He'll show you how

Let him catch you by hand

He will lead you to that promise land

My Vacation

When time has come and I must go

And no longer my faith to show

Just to hear my master call

Come my child and live with me

I will show you around eternity

Then I will bow my head and say goodnight

And I will get ready to take my heavenly flight

Everything will be all right

If we let Jesus, our battles win

Put your problems in his hands

He will always understand

I found out a long time ago

When I had no place to go

It must be a place somewhere up there

Where God is always in charge of every care

It must be beautiful too

For there is no more dying

In that land so bright and fair

There is no more grief or cares

And if I spend a million years

I will not shed a single tear

I will be so happy to be home

Never again will I be alone

As I look into his radiant face

And he will share his loving grace

After all These Years

Lord you have blessed me for 75 years

I can't say that I haven't shed a tear

Neither can I say that I have no fears

After all these years

For you have walked with me all the way

Many times I've had to stop and pray

But you would show me the way

After all these years

For you have walked with me all my the way

Many times I've had to stop and pray

But you would show me the way

After all these years

When you would show me the way

And you would make my day clear

Then I would no fear

For God was near

And all of doubt has disappeared

After all of these years

When you are with me

Everything seems bright

For it then, that I can see the light

When I spend time with God

After all these years

Sometimes I get confused

My journey isn't always bright

Sometimes it seems as if there is no light

Put your trust in God

For it will then be all right

If you walk with Jesus he will make it all right

For we walk by faith

And not by sight

I get so confused sometimes

I don't clearly understand

God's wonderful plan

That he so willingly made it for man

Then I bowed on my knees

And this is what I had to say

God, what would you have me to do today?

For I only want to do it your way

Lord will you take my hand

And try and make me understand

All about your wonderful plan

Then he took me by the hand

And helped me to understand

All about his wonderful plan

God has something on his mind

God has something on his mind

He will prepare you for a certain time

Whatever you do with your life

Give it to God

And you will be surprised

If you live for him and be true

He will always look out for you

If you keep him on your mind

You will love him all the time

And if you serve him night and day

You will learn how to pray

But if you invite him to come in your heart

He will be with you until the end

God never forgets us for he never sleeps

He always love us and he will always be there

And he will meet our needs

God is a spirit and he is always true

He never forgets us, whatever we do

For he loves us all the time

And he keeps us on his mind

Sinful man

To the sinful man, who simply can't understand?

God's will for you and me

He did it so we might be free

And live with him for eternity

O sinful man what is your plan?

I know a man that holds the sand

He made it simple

Just invite him into your heart

Then you will see, just where to start

O sinful man what is your plan?

For it has surely changed for the better

O sinful man, who had no plan

This is where you now stand

Take God's hand and hold on to it as tight as you can

Keep looking forward never looking back

And when you hear his mighty call

He will say

Come on up

This where you'll stay

So again you are faced, with an opportunity that remains

If you will, have no shame

Get on your knees and ask him

Lord forgive a sinner

Lord please makes me a winner

Deliver me, uphold me

For surely I will be

With you in Kingdom

For eternity

I've got to know I'm saved

Living in these latter days

I have got to know that I am saved

I must prepare to meet my God

I must do it while I yet live

Then on that day I will have no fear

I am sure in the end; God will forgive us from our sins

So do it now while you have plenty of time

And he will always keep you in mind

And he will bless you all your days

If you give him love and praise then he will give

You truth and grace and your sorrows he will erase

Our first Christmas away from home

It was early one Christmas morning and I was awakened by the beautiful

Morning sunlight gleaming through my window

As I lay there suddenly I remembered, I was a long way from home

In my mind I began to wonder what I had done wrong by being

So far away from home my husband and I had taken this trip

Out of true- friendship

Knowing our children had gone

And leaving us all alone

This was the very first Christmas we spent away from our home

When our children were there we did not have a single care

There were nuts, fruits, and candies to spare

With turkey and dressing, pies, and cakes

Everyone was anxious and could hardly wait

Knowing our children had gone leaving us all alone

This was the first Christmas we spent away from home

Then a voice spoke silently to me it said, "Let them all be free

For this is time that God gave you, that you must be alone

For much of your time you spent on them

Now it is for you to do for yourself

What you must do and be thankful you done your part

It takes a load off of your heart

Because God knows that you have done your part

So leave the rest in his hands

Be thankful to God and share his joy with others

Will you live for God?

Jesus came from his home alone

He gave his life for you and me

For that reason I am free

He will always do his part

It is in your heart to serve God

Turn from your wicked ways

He will help you if you say

Please forgive me for my sins

"Don't leave me behind

And will you serve all the time?

If you learn to sing to pray

And live your life for him each day

You will be blessed in every way

No better time than now to start

For God always knows, what's in your heart

God Understands

In the fall of October on very gloomy day

I stood looking out the window and wondered

To myself what could I say?

As I gazed into the skies I saw

The beautiful clouds roll by

The trees shaded with green leaves

As the wind pass by

The sun peeped in and out the white

Crimson clouds and kiss the summer good bye

I hardly knew what to do

Somehow I wanted to cry

What a beautiful day to feel this way

God is the reason, and why many times in

Life things happen, we don't know why?

But only God knows what is in my heart why not?

Kneel down and pray and he will answer in the end

And this is what he will say

I love you my child with all my heart

So you have a good day.

Spring time

Of all the seasons of the year

I think that spring is the best

Its brings forth all kinds of weather and

It's different from the rest

Its brings the rain and storms sometimes fires too

Sometimes I get afraid and

Don't know what to do

Before you count spring out

Listen to what I say

Spring can make summer's day smile

It can make the cold days

Warm weather it makes the spring better

It shares with us warm weather and breezes

And quite slow rains and the sun peeps through

The clouds and let you know its spring.

God has all power

God has all power in his hands

Even though we may not understand

It is not by might and not by faith

But by my spirit says, the Lord

We must serve him and read his word

To understand God's plan

That he has made known to all man

Then you will fully understand

God is the reason we must trust his plan

For he has all power in his hands he laid down his life

For sinful man so that we might understand

His plan means so much to me

Lord please, take me by the hand

Lead me to the promise land

If I trust him with my life

I want have to pay the price

If I live in his presence each day

There will be no price to pay

If I can hold on

If you can just hold onto God

He will never leave you all alone

Why not let him have his way?

For he will meet you each and every day

He will always hear your call

And never let you fall and he knows

You are his friend he will stand by

You too until the end

If you find the time each day

Bow on your knees and pray

And mean it from your heart

Then, he will give you a new start

If you feel all alone and lose your strength

To hold on! He will keep you in his care

And he will help you realize he is everywhere

He will always be there to answer your prayers

God's grace

Through God's grace and truth

Christ did it all for you and me

He gave his life upon the cross

So you and I may not be lost

For someone as great as he

Who gave his life on Calvary?

Only God with such a love

Would leave his home from up above

He came to carry out a plan

Which was made by his father's hand?

Because he came and died for me

Grace and Truth have set me free

Glenda posing for the camera at a friend's house in (2007)

Here's a picture of me posing for a picture in 1986.

Right to left: Brenda, Glenda, Linda
Me & my 2 older sisters sitting on my dad's favorite car .

Glenda enjoying listening to a local jazz band in the park.(1986)

Jolie

Little child playing on the swing

Laughing and singing and doing her own thing

Her eyes are big and she wears a smile

I can picture her running through the park

With her arms held high

Waving at strangers as they pass her by

She's animated vigorous and a lot of fun

Her laughter is contagious but her personality is bold.

I wouldn't trade this girl for silver or gold.

I Remember

I remember when you were a child the way you laughed and flashed your smile

I remember the day you took your first- step you grinned in spite of yourself

I remember when your baby tooth fell – out and you hid it under your pillow

I remember when a bully ridiculed you and chased you home

The tears you shed because you felt all alone

I remember your first- heart – break and how you promised to never make that mistake

I remember the day you got married the first – time you pushed Jolie's baby carriage

I remember when you got your first apartment and wasn't too sure about living on your own.

I remember when you got your first car you thought you were cool like a movie star.

I remember obstacles you have to overcome to become the man you are today.

I am proud of you and I must say. I thank God for your gracious style.

And most of all I thank God that you still have that big flashy smile.

By: Glenda Bagley

Time

Time cannot be measured in dollars and cents

Your time on this earth will be wasted if not well spent

Time is a gift from God he gives us all

It doesn't matter if you are large or small, fat or tall

We should take the time to save a lost soul

Change a young life in a world so cold

The days, months, and years pass so quickly

The time we all have may not be long

Invest your life do not waste it

Because someday your time too will be gone

By: Glenda Bagley

I Dream

I dream of a place where there is no grief

Where everyone is accepted and there's endless peace

I dream of a place where hope can grow.

A place where a child will always have a safe place to go

I dream of a place where tranquility and faith transcends

I dream of a place where life never ends

I dream of a place where people are renewed regenerated and fulfilled

I dream of a place where God will harvest all souls

By: Glenda Bagley

Little Boy!

Little boy with your arms out- stretched who are you waiting for?

Let me guess? Standing there in the tall green grass with your blue jeans worn tightly

Winter is coming now that summer has gone I do miss your warm and gentle smile

Your soft little hands and your peculiar style

You made me laugh, you made me grin I prayed to God that would someday meet again

You were a quiet child who often kept to yourself

Small in stature but always exploring

In your career you travelled the world to serve your country.

Time has moved on and you have a little boy of your very own

I can picture him with the same little out- stretched arms and tiny hands

Waiting for you to visit him to that little boy Roy that I once knew

I want to say that I am proud of you! I am proud of the good strong man you are today

I say, embrace that little boy who stood all alone in the tall green grass

Love him because he has developed to be a loving and confident man

By: Glenda Bagley

To Savannah with love

This small city has an echo of harmony

It's beautiful yet quiet

The people are so friendly the food is Um! Um! good

I wish I could stay here a lot longer Oh! I certainly would

The beautiful warm beaches the tall plush grass

Oh, how I wish my vacation could last

If you want to taste southern cuisine this is the place to go

Ask any resident they will surly say so

The restaurants are small and quaint,

I may not know exactly where I am but I know where I ain't

The houses are so beautiful the trees are tall and so green

If you don't believe me go and visit you'll see what I mean

Here is a picture of a house in Savannah where my relatives live.

I grew – up in a small town in West Texas my 9 siblings and I. We shared some good times and even some bad.

But the love of our parents we always had. They taught us the principles of the Bible and disciplined us when needed. Looking back I can that we were not the "Perfect family. But I had a precious gift from God two parents that loved me unconditionally. Now, that I am 47 years old I treasure the memories of the times we spent together

In that small 3 bedroom house where I was loved and treasured because there truly is no place like home.

My mother always said, that in life everyone has a purpose in life. Something that God assigns us to do while here on earth. We all must find what God's purpose is for us.

Romans 8: 28 says

And we know that all things work together for good to them that love God , to them who are the called according to his purpose. Somehow I knew that I was loved by my parents. Love that was unconditional who could ask for more.

Home

There's no place like home no matter where one travels or roams

There's no place like your child hood home

No other place where you can be protected

Where's there is love and you're not neglected

A place where you can get a home cooked meals

A place where your broken heart can be healed

Home is a place where love prevails

Let me tell you home is where all is well

By: Glenda Bagley

This is a photograph of the house I lived in as a child.

The Bagley Family: left to right Rodney Linda Walker Glenda Joe, Lee Bagley Sr., Lovella, Lee Bagley Jr ,Charles, Willis, Michael, Tarsha, Brenda Davis pictured posing with their parents as they renew their wedding vows. (July 23, 1994)

The End